FAR SIDE OF
THE EARTH

BOOKS BY TOM SLEIGH

After One

Waking

The Chain

The Dreamhouse

Herakles, by Euripides
    (TRANSLATION)

FAR SIDE
of the EARTH

Tom Sleigh

A Mariner Book

HOUGHTON MIFFLIN COMPANY

BOSTON | NEW YORK

First Mariner Books edition 2005

Copyright © 2003 by Tom Sleigh

Visit our Web site: www.houghtonmifflinbooks.com.

Library of Congress Cataloging-in-Publication Data
Sleigh, Tom.
Far side of the earth / Tom Sleigh.
p. cm.
ISBN 0-618-30242-5
ISBN 0-618-49238-0 (pbk.)
1. Title.
PS3569.L36F37 2003
811'.54—dc21   2002191294

Book design by Melissa Lotfy

Printed in the United States of America

QUM 10 9 8 7 6 5 4 3 2 1

Grateful acknowledgment is made to the following publications in which many of these poems first appeared: *Agni:* "Amores, II, vi," "Amores, III, ix." *The Bread Loaf Anthology of Contemporary American Poetry:* "Spring Morning," "Joy on a Sunday" (reprinted from *Slate*). *Dia Center for the Arts:* "To Water," "To Dust" (printed as a broadside). *Raritan:* "On the Soul of a Flea," "To Water." *Slate:* "Joy on a Sunday," "Crosswalk." *Tikkun:* "Interrogation." *Tin House:* "Day Room," "On the Yard," "Cannibal Love." *Threepenny:* "Bridge." *TriQuarterly:* "Newsreel," "For Robert Owen Sleigh, P.F.C., 100th Division," "Tracks," "Nomad," "Trees by Firelight," "This Day Only," "After a Long Illness," "The Fissure," "New York American Spell, 2001." *Yale Review:* "What Can Be Said."

I would like to thank the Poetry Society of America for the financial support provided by the Shelley Memorial Award.

This book is for the members of my family: Ellen, Tim, Owen and Virginia, Rosamond, young Owen, Jay and Mary, and the Rowes and the Driscolls.

CONTENTS

FAR SIDE OF
THE EARTH

Interrogation

We began
to interrogate each image for the promise of meaning
we needed to believe in

in order to hold out
against the wheel we were bound to
and enthralled by—

we were children of earth, sun, of the drugged eye of Mars.

We were frightened of our own need of origin—
we wanted malleable clay
not granite . . .

But we sat at the table separating us
and tried to make love a lens
that would focus our past errors
surrounding us like Medusa's forest of stone men and women
frozen in attitudes of flight and anger . . .

But it was necessary to learn
every gesture and transmute it into ourselves
to refute our sentimental questions, arid investigations,
the smaller and smaller truths
we fossilized around.

And unlearning
was a learning more arduous
and different than the lineaments of a stone hand reaching out
caught in a seizure
that could be a caress.

I

Tracks

for Jin Soo Kim

Evanescent engine in its ether-housing,
The soul pulls out from the Depot of Unknowing:

Moment outside time, moment of pure relation
Where coils of nerves lit up like bare bulbs

Glow all night in the abandoned station . . .
No conductor, no tickets, no golden spike

Glinting in the desert where track meets track,
No signal, warning beacon, no switch or switchman,

No boxcar, caboose, flange, no piston,
Nothing but the soul's own eccentric motion

Along rails converging to a vanishing point . . .
Beyond that point the Museum of the Invisible

Holds spirits from Lódź, Vilna, Warsaw,
Riding the rails to where the rails sink out of sight . . .

Spirit of Matter, casual anti-angel
Whose smile or frown means that we live or die,

Your will racing at the speed of thought
And carving through chaos and inanition

And the finest shadings of space and earth
Can't catch that tiny, brave, flickering

Engine that keeps improvising its destination
On dissolving wheels of smoke unstoppably

Arriving each moment at each nowhere junction.

Newsreel

It was like being in the crosshairs of a magnifying glass
Or the beams of the planets concentrating in a death ray
Passing right through me, boring a hole between

My shoes through the concrete floor all the way
To the far side of the earth. Yet it was only
Not knowing how to get where I was going,

I'd gotten lost in the parking lot on the way
To the cinderblock bunker where my mother
Worked the snack bar, my father the projector.

The drive-in movie screen stretched horizon
To horizon, the whole of Texas sprawled around,
Cathedral-like De Sotos and great-finned Pontiacs

Flickering and sinister in torrents of light flooding
Down the screen. Frozen in that light, I
Might have been the disconsolate ageless

Stone-eyed child ornamenting a pillar
In a dead Roman city high up on a desert plateau.
I wasn't even as tall as the speakers mumbling

On and on the way now in my dream of extreme
Old age I hear voices mumbling interminably . . .
Where does it shimmer, my refuge, grotto of my swimming pool

Lapping in the infinite leisure of the newsreel?
At last my mother appeared from among the cars
And led me back to the snack bar but I still hovered

Out there, turned loose among the shadows'
Disembodied passions striving for mastery
Above the tensed windshields: There gleams

Marilyn Monroe movie star enjoying her fame
In the voluptuous, eternal present tense
Of celebrity being worked over by hands

Of her masseur. Bougainvillea overgrows
Her beach bungalow retreat of peace and pleasure,
The screen nothing now but layer on layer

Of flesh the fingers knead in a delirious ballet
Pushing, pulling, palms slippery and quick,
Ambiguous instruments of comfort or of pain.

The rush of blood to her face clouds into
White light as film stock jerks across
A void half coma blackout, half nightmare aura:

The film jammed, raw light pulsing like a bandage
On a face wrapped round and round in surgical gauze.
Wherever that light took me looms far from candy bars

And gum wrappers blazing under glass. The movie poster
Death ray stopped the earth revolving, time had stopped,
My mother's black slacks and my father's not yet grown goatee,

My own hands shaking nervously about were silently dissolving
In that ray bombarding from beyond the galaxy
Being invaded by screeching, beseeching noises

Of alien beings searching for a planetary home.
Then, up there, on the screen, frenetic in the light,
Was a hair trembling between two cloven lobes

Of shadow that were part of the projector's
Overheating brain, its brilliantly babbling, delusional,
Possessed by shadows, dispossessed brain.

Day Room

His head rose like a torch in a tomb.
Banquet-style, as at a second Symposium,

The others lounged on couches or lay knocked out.
A net of shadows dangled from wire-meshed windows.

Buffeted there, there, some swam against currents
Or were swept off into underwater canyons.

Visitors, confusion streaming over them, speech
Foaming into eddies, words lolling like jetsam

On the lightless bottom, listened to the news
Of minds crammed in bodies: Here, all was stoic

Or hectic or unspeaking disconnection.
Moving shadows on the TV screen implied

A world out there, though a world more couth,
More uncouth? in four o'clock's slushy freezing dark:

Plato's cave loomed in semblance of the walls,
Only wasn't it the cave as All, no outside

Not inside, nothing more real to go out into?
He peered far down to where dark swam up

From the depthless screen and hovered poised
Above dark-in-light: Sergeant Schultz kept repeating,

"I know nothing, nothing," his funny-Nazi German accent
As he recoils from his ever suave tormentor, the American

POW Colonel Hogan who threatens Schultz
With good-humored ruthlessness as bad as a mother

In a supermarket aisle cajoling her greedy-eyed child,
"Ah ah ah — remember the Russian front!"

— Poor Schultz's accent making him more human in his terror,
Though only an actor acting his lines through

The canned laughter's bacchic furor sweeping down
The corridor to die in murmurs of slippers shushing.

Cast yourself in it, imagine having to say those lines,
Not just now, but always, eternity a chaos

Of laugh-track frenzy more demonic than funny,
Reruns of Hogan haunted by the actor

Who acts Hogan's lines, his real-life orgies
Before a secret camera ending in his Golgotha,

His infamy to be bludgeoned and found wrapped
Naked in a shower curtain that hangs

In the mind like the cave's walls turning outside
Inside outside inside no end or difference inside out

—The almost see-through membrane of a world gone flat:
He hunches forward to change the channel,

Muttering something to Schultz's "I know nothing, nothing,"
A grim joke maybe, "Ain't that the truth . . ." though really,

Who could know what words he was or wasn't
Answering, who can hear above the roar of

Earth moving under him, trying to throw him off
As he clings to the sofa hurtling through space!

And as he clings, the screen slowly opens and fans out wide
Around the National Broadcasting Corporation peacock

Waving its plumes, flaming blues, greens, radiant vermilions,
Brilliance of the seasons, late-morning pastels

Easy and restful for the brain and eye,
Sempiternal hues Atlantis rose up and sank back into.

And these feather off into grays, solid wintry
Grays that give off nothing and reflect nothing back.

Crosswalk

Nakedness of air, raiment of words.
Tarred cornices burnished by streetlight.
He, she, passing in the night; my own shadow

Refuting substance, me my own ghost—
The city around me shrinking, lost . . .
And then this woman—her small steps eroding

White lines from asphalt, a scratch faintly bleeding
On her forehead, her pleasure in dragging
On her cigarette; not phantom, not wife

Or adorer of Ammon, simply she
In her cotton dress, rosettes asserting
Her eye for color, form . . . Where they dump the city's

Garbage, in the Kills, they throw me in, not knowing
I am soul too, soul hovering in limbo:
I wait, I struggle: Where is the zone,

Imperishable, I must enter?
Moulage head of a god talking in a dream,
Ruler and judge weighing out my heart

On the balance pan, pointing to the staircase
I must climb—and then the old woman
Came into sight: Both of us at the crosswalk,

Traffic blurring by us, fuming
Flurry of ghosts. I want to speak to her,
Ask my way as she navigates through

Glare, eyes fixed on the gutter opposite:
Naked soul in space that opens into
Absence, soul that can speak to no one,

Nothing, soul that seeks to find "justified"
Glyphed beside its earthly name! . . .
Through her, the city shines immersed in light,

Trash, plane trees budding. I turn the corner
Into the innermost chamber where
Sculpted on its western wall is a door

We dead pass through to share offerings
Brought by the pious living — natron
And asphalt to preserve flesh, mask of linen

And stucco on the face, winding swaths of
Linen bandages — but I was poor, poor
In body and had to make shift in a simple grave,

Body enveloped by only a few rags
Encased in a rough wooden coffin . . .
— Old woman in the street, you walk through me,

I am ravished by you, your lavish
Gardenia musky smell, your white nurse's
Shoes, your burnt down to the butt cigarette.

On the Yard

After lockdown, tier by tier undresses to sleep:
Each skull nestles in its mattress-hollow.
Wall facing wall inside of wall shrinks to a keyhole:
A fly creeps through and starts to buzz, reeling through bars
Down steel corridors. A dreamer's eye follows the fly,
And wherever the fly lands, the eye touches down
With an airier Midas touch that turns all to glass:
The eye wakes to Bentham's panopticon, glazed cage
Of an inspection house where only the Warden sees all.

—I am asleep and not asleep,
I stare up into faces swarming:

Cellblocks of memory focus face by face,
Mine flitting in and out of theirs: In prison issue
They come, footsteps mingling over mine in a child's game
Of chase from yard to cell, only we're all grown men,
Meatier, less and more malign than
A boy's imagining himself grown . . .

—I was asleep and not asleep,
Faces came and went.

Frank the Joker, the West Virginia biker, who composed
"A rhyme to fit the crime":
"There was a young fellow named Frank
Who gave his girlfriend a spank;
She fell in a heap

In front of Frank's jeep
And old Frank ran her down for a prank."

Or the white-haired lifer, densely oracular:
"Sometimes, after lockdown, your thoughts
Just don't have the energy to climb the wall."

The Giggler who bolted
His brother in a barn and burned it down,
Eyes challenging, sly:
"They killed this guy and see, I think this is funny, hilarious
In fact, but you, you won't think so — they cut off his dick
And shoved it in his mouth."

Or the child molester who said about flowers
At funerals: "They're there, aren't they,
To hide the stink off the corpse?"

Or Pat, armed robber
Who held aloof: Rolled shirtsleeves, forearms
Carved from basalt, smoke rings
Lazily effusing:
"The johns here, they got no doors:
You ever try to take a shit while someone's watching?
It took six months to get used to that —
But here, man, the bars feed on
Time, they nibble
It to nothing."

—I wanted to sleep and couldn't sleep,
I stared up into faces swarming.

Three o'clock dark dissolves
The walls, faces start to drift, their atoms
Mix with concrete's
Atomic swirl, bodies get stuck
Floating halfway through, heartbeats
Booming as through a stethoscope:

Like Michelangelo's slaves, if a fly
Landed on their noses,
They couldn't lift a hand to brush it off.

Dark velleities buzz in this hive of steel
Where power handshakes
Flower in forests
Of interlocking fingers:

In red prison uniform, a man
On death row, convicted 1984, exonerated and pardoned
October 2000 (*New York Times,* Dec. 10):
"You could hear the humming of the chair
Every time they cut it on, like an air-conditioner
Cutting on. My daddy came to see me, he said, 'What's that?'
I said, 'The chair.' The way they put it, they got to test the chair."

—I was asleep
And couldn't wake up.

Inside my skull, glass
Keeps shattering: Dream-beings
Unsubjected to the will, with insect bodies
And human heads, dash against walls, mammal softness

Of cheeks and lips join with stingers
Pulsing . . . my eyes awake and not awake, where is the chamber
As in the horror movie *Return of the Fly* that, circuitry and test-tubes
Sparking, would unscramble these divided
Natures?

(They called me "Teach"
As in "Hey, Teach, how do you spell . . ."
When I confessed I'd been to jail, they looked disappointed in me:
Their side of the wall was theirs, not mine.)

—I tried to turn over, to look away,
But couldn't wake up, couldn't not wake.

Chemicals drip into a man's veins, one each
For heart, lungs, brain.
Strapped to a table, he stares
Impassive, eyes flickering shut, body
A meat wall, IV tubes
Almost empty . . .

—I was asleep and not asleep,
I couldn't move to wake.

I hear shrill wings—that fly inspecting bread crumbs
Under dining hall tables while the Warden blares
Descartes over the Intercom:
"If a man's head were lopped off
His mouth would keep on moving, faultlessly
Justifying his crimes."

But that fly, that speck against
Steel, its wings steered in ways that seem crazy
To eyes awake, not awake,
Not seeing, all-seeing, the head unmoving
Moving to turn away . . . oh seely fly
I can't not see, can't move to brush away
From my unsleeping eyes, you veer
In spirals unflattened into pathos
Of careening chaos, your eccentric
Flight path darts
Through bars, oh alas, hairy
Vibrant fly!

On the Soul of a Flea

Bloodsucker. Plague carrier. Scourge
Of prisoners and the poor.
Prince of itches who thrives in our dirty world.

Blake saw
Your soul somersaulting
Out of your body:
Face of a space alien. Torso of an acrobat.
Fingers and toes
Curving into spiraling claws.

Ellis Island. Hell's Kitchen. Watts. South Boston.
The riots in Jerusalem when Christ entered on a donkey
And reached down to scratch his ankle
As the donkey twitched an ear.

The sleeve that wrote: ". . . Being unwell, fleabit,
I was quite downcast: Nature in all her parcels and faculties
Gaped and fell apart
Like a clod cleaving and holding only
By strings of roots."

A young recruit noted
To his mother and aunt: "The fleas are as bad
As you can think. We had bayonet practice, which I did fine at,
Though the targets are made of straw and infested
With fleas. God knows they bite and bite us."

"Fleaness." Your own peculiar "fleaness."

The flea's penchant, like a lover's,
For this body over that one,
Its distinct savor and odor
Winking and bubbling at the brim.

Suffering seen up close, death up close:

Tumbling into
The invisible, a flea's soul
Demands initiation into mysteries,
Lush pharmacopoeias
And their intricate side effects,
The speech of angels and devils
Real as the *Physicians' Desk Reference.*

What does a flea possess
But its host's blood, its pride at jumping
Through fire and its death-defying tricks
On the trapeze?

Flea, will you be there, biting us
Back to consciousness, your appetite
Keeping us aloft
As we wirewalk above our flesh dissolving
Into nothingness?

Companion of the fly the poet heard
Just as she died.

Ready spirit who bit Odysseus' old dog
To wake him from his stupor
And wag his tail for the familiar beggar at the door.

Ice Age

Noises like the sound of the ice pack breaking up.
A calving iceberg drifting toward the future.

An icy guttural howling raving in the wind.
Then the avalanche in slow motion came floating down.

Eyes, mouth closed against whiteout blizzarding,
Everything buried deep . . . Then chisels and snow axes

Chip his body from the ice, body frozen nine thousand years,
Body kept cold in a refrigerated tank of glass

So whoever on the research team can look just when they want,
Yes, conjecturing this and that, the body on the slab

Hunched over on its side as if choking
With laughter the way someone at a party

Might fall down laughing and everyone will look,
Only nobody knows what the joke's about.

How can the ice man, after nine thousand years
Of such hilarity, recover enough

Composure to tell the joke? Could it be
The one about the cave, where everything

Is a shadow until you step outside and see
What casts the shadow? Or the alternate

Punch line, in which every life is a shadow life,
With whatever casts the shadow hidden out of sight?

One of his prehistoric kind, to let out demon pain,
Expertly trepanned a hole in his skull;

His groin is shriveled, the sack of scrotum
Shines like leather, the coils of his last shit

Reveal his last meal consisted of a little barley
And painkilling herbs for his cracked arthritic rib.

Near to where they dug him out is a mass grave,
The forensics establishing that "multiple blows

With hammerlike implements had penetrated
Many of the victims' frontal bones, with fracture lines

Radiating out from this penetration,
And that often another second injury,

Consisting of a depressed skull fracture
Of the outer layer of the cranial vault,

As well as many clean fractures through
The zygomatic arch were the cause of death."

After fleeing the massacre, was he lying down
To rest when the avalanche covered him?

Was he simply out hunting and got tired
And froze to death? Curled on his right side

To spare him pain in his left, after his long,
Uneventful passage of ice and wind and snow,

His hand was still clutching a bow which
Only a man of great strength could have bent . . .

Cold is the marrow of all knowing;
Ice can be shaved as fine as what is thought.

In the way I was conjecturing it,
In the way I was thinking it through and through,

In the way in which I heard or imagined
I heard a subtle whispering in the wind,

That was the way the ice man told me his joke,
With a punch line I couldn't possibly understand.

Nomad

My first impulse was to want to see her peaceful;
But she sat at the bottom of a well, far off,
And kept talking "the world," its wars and child-soldiers

Firing off machine guns, all of it removed
Though, pixilated on a screen and so devolving
From the real: Her mind was magnetized

To disaster as once it was attracted
To quiet and study — but no longer, not anymore:
The sun shining in her face seemed to negate her,

The moon she talked down the sky each night
Crushed her beneath its banal pallor:
Absence like presence diffused through her kitchen,

In her housecoat she was the familiar of a cloud
Of particles that one moment coalesced
Into friends and a husband of forty years,

Then shattered apart, speeding away from each other faster
And faster. She kept repeating, "The President
Needs to understand that these children are confused,

They're numb somehow, they don't comprehend killing."
Her impassive eyes and long-jawed face
Wore the expression of a nomad and her horse

Journeying into the *chott* that closes in behind them . . .
Meanwhile, digging trenches in her ear, 737s rumbled over —
Everything seemed suspended, the furniture

Nicked and stuffing falling out among columns
Of house dust radiantly revolving
And drifting white dog hair from the dog licking

And licking at her hand. The Count Basie disk
She played over and over, notes
Doubling back and echoing higher up the scale,

Brasses booming and wambling in the dusk,
Drumsticks scorching the high hat and the snare,
Reverberated down into her well shaft —

Hot winds and sand wailing through the kitchen,
She'd traveled beyond benign reflection
And reveled in exaltation of her thought:

She was Lawrence of Arabia confessing
To her blank listener and the TV murmuring,
Blood is always on our hands: We are licensed to it.

Then her eyes became the well shaft sunk
So deep it tapped into ice aboriginal,
Infernal, ice that freezes round the dead.

As she talked, talked, I saw ice run
And crack, trickle to streams that soon
Would overflow and release the body

Of a child-soldier stepping forth
To lead her off, his teeth, when he smiled,
Showing a little crooked, warning her

Fuck all that, stop all that talking,
Where we're going we won't need any talking,
But her mouth kept moving, already she was savoring

That wholly different and arid light and air.

New York American Spell, 2001

What was going on in the New York American
Black/red/green helmeted neon night?
The elevator door was closing behind us, we were the ones

Plunging floor after floor after floor after floor
To the abyss — but it was someone else's face
Staring from the screen out at us, someone else's face

Saying something flashing from the teleprompter:
Though what the face said was meant to reassure,
Down in the abyss the footage kept playing,

All of it looping back like children chanting
The answers to nonsensical riddles, taunting
A classmate who doesn't know the question:

"Because it's too far to walk" "Time to get a new fence"
"A big red rock eater." And as the images rewound
And the face kept talking, the clear night sky

Filled up with smoke and the smoke kept pouring
Itself out into the air like a voice saying something
It can't stop saying, some murky omen

Like schoolkids asking: "Why do birds fly south?"
"What time is it when an elephant sits on the fence?"
"What's big, red, and eats rocks?"

A woman hugging another woman
Who was weeping blocked the sidewalk.
Nobody moved for a moment.

They were an island caught at the tide turning:
Such misery in two human bodies.

Then the wearing away of the crowd
Moving flowed over them and they
Were pulled swiftly along down the sidewalk.

Faces powdered with dust and ash, there they were
In the fast food place, raucous and wild, splitting
The seams of their work clothes, weary to hysteria

As they hunched in their booth next to the buffet
Under heat lamps reflecting incarnadine
Off pastas and vegetable slag. Then the joke

Ignited, they quivered on the launch pad,
Laughter closed around them, they couldn't
Breathe, it was as if they were staring out

From a space capsule porthole and were asking
The void an imponderable riddle
While orbiting so high up in space

That the earth was less than the least hint
Of light piercing the smoke-filled, cloudless night.
(What was the joke about? Nobody knew.)

And then they stopped laughing and stared into their plates,
Ash smearing down their faces as they chewed.

4 / SPELL SPOKEN BY SUPPLIANT TO HELIOS
FOR KNOWLEDGE
from the Greek Magical Papyri

Under my tongue is the mud of the Nile,
I wear the baboon hide of sacred Keph.
Dressed in the god's power, I am the god,
I am Thouth, discoverer of healing drugs,
Founder of letters. As god calls on god
I summon you to come to me, you
Under the earth; arouse yourself for me,
Great daimon, you the subterranean,
You of the primordial abyss.
Unless you tell me what I want to know,
What is in the minds of everyone, Egyptians,
Greeks, Syrians, Ethiopians, of every race
And people, unless I know what has been
And what shall be, unless I know their skills
And practices and works and lives and names
Of them and their fathers and mothers
And brothers and friends, even of those now dead,
I will pour the blood of the black-faced jackal
As an offering in a new-made jar and put it
In the fire and burn beneath it what's left
Of the bones of all-praised Osiris,
And I will shout in the port of Busiris
The secrets of his mysteries, that his body,
Drowned, remained in the river three days
And three nights, that he, the praised one,
Was carried by the river into the sea
And surrounded by wave on wave on wave

And by mist rising off water through the air.
To keep your belly from being eaten by fish,
To keep the fish from chewing your flesh with their mouths,
To make the fish close their hungry jaws, to keep
The fatherless child from being taken
From his mother, to keep the pole of the sky
From being brought down and the twin towering
Mountains from toppling into one, to keep Anoixis
From running amok and doing just what she wants,
Not god or goddess will give oracles
Until I know through and through
Just what is in the minds of all human beings,
Egyptians, Syrians, Greeks, Ethiopians, of every race
And people, so that those who come to me,
Their eyes and mine can meet in a level gaze,
Neither one or the other higher or lower,
And whether they speak or keep silent,
I can tell them whatever has happened
And is happening and is going to happen
To them, and I can tell them their skills
And their works and their names and those of their dead,
And of every human being who comes to me
I will read them as I read a sealed letter
And tell them everything truthfully.

Sun shines on the third bridge tower:
A garbage scow ploughs the water,

Maternal hull pushing it all out beyond
The city, pushing it all out so patiently—

All you could hear out there this flawless afternoon
Is the sound of sand pulverizing newsprint

To tatters, paper-pulp ripping crosswise
Or lengthwise, shearing off some photo

Of maybe a head or maybe an arm.
Ridiculous flimsy noble newspaper,

Leaping in wind, fluttering, collapsing,
Its columns sway and topple into babble:

All you'd see if you were out there
Is air vanishing into clearer air.

Pressed against our seats, then released to air,
From the little plane windows we peered four thousand feet
Down to the ground desert-gray and still,
Nothing seeming to be moving on that perfect afternoon,
No reminder of why it was we were all looking,
Remembering maybe the oh so flimsy
Wooden sawhorse police barricades, as the woman
In front of me twisted her head back to see
It all again, but up there there was nothing to see,
Only the reef water feel of transparency
Deepening down to a depth where everything
Goes dark and nothing moves unless it belongs
To that dark, darting in and out or undulating
Slowly or cruising unblinking, jaws open or closed.

from the Greek Magical Papyri

This is the charm that will protect you, the charm
That you must wear: Onto lime wood write
With vermilion the secret name, name of
The fifty magic letters. Then say the words:
"Guard me from every daimon of the air,
On the earth and under the earth, guard me
From every angel and phantom, every
Ghostly visitation and enchantment,
Me, your suppliant." Enclose it in a skin
Dyed purple, hang it round your neck and wear it.

Vines of smoke through the latticework of steel
Weave the air into a garden of smoke.

And in the garden people came and went,
People of smoke and people of flesh, the air dressed

In ash. What the pictures couldn't say
Was spoken by the smoke: A common language

In a tongue of smoke that murmured in every ear
Something about what it was they'd been forced

To endure: Words spoken in duress,
Inconsolable words, words spoken under the earth

That rooted in smoke and breathed in the smoke
And put forth shoots that twined through the steel,

Words plunged through the roof of the garages'
Voids, I-beams twisted; the eye that saw all this

Tells and tells again one part of the story
Of that day of wandering through the fatal garden,

The camera's eye open and acutely
Recording in the foul-smelling air.

from a Sumerian spell, 2000 B.C.

Like molten bronze and iron shed blood
        pools. Our country's dead
melt into the earth
        as grease melts in the sun, men whose
helmets now lie scattered, men annihilated

by the double-bladed axe. Heavy, beyond
        help, they lie still as a gazelle
exhausted in a trap,
        muzzle in the dust. In home
after home, empty doorways frame the absence

of mothers and fathers who vanished
        in the flames remorselessly
spreading claiming even
        frightened children who lay quiet
in their mother's arms, now borne into

oblivion, like swimmers swept out to sea
        by the surging current.
May the great barred gate
        of blackest night again swing shut
on silent hinges. Destroyed in its turn,

may this disaster too be torn out of mind.

Joy on a Sunday

Pulsing there like a wound in the air
       Turning to a mouth that sings what
My parents in their thirty-fourth year
       So loved to hear in her throat—
There are so many reasons they could offer:
       The delayed pain of war
         In the bedroom,
The sorrow that "many boys didn't come home . . ."
       Joy on a Sunday
Morning to hear her voice, palpable, throaty,
       Enjoying the immense
       Obstacles overcome the way love,
       Abrasive and intense
Even when it hungers in shadows
       Dissatisfied, breasts bulwarks of
         Lips and eyes.
Mother, Father, they're downstairs listening
       To Judy Garland sing,
       Zing went the strings of my heart
       Clang clang clang went the trolley
       The man that got away . . .
How unendurably sweet and perfect
       Is her tone!—
Though the undertones are raw, raw to the bone
       The lacerating flair
       Of her makeshift mastery, her voice
       Shredding into rags she wore

Like finery,
Casting off the old Judy
And no reason
Or clichés about wars
Suffice.
Mother, Father, and Judy together,
United in
Their momentary rapture,
Seated on a couch in orbit through the stars,
Look down on all that happens
And will happen
And keeps on
Happening while the record turns.

II

Cannibal Love
after Ovid

What purpose of the world's were we all serving?

Love's light swiveled horizon to horizon,
Illuminating fields where both sexes,
All persuasions were encamped, the rumor
Love was a cannibal drifter ready
To carve devotees to cutlets stirring
No paranoia in that commingling
Of bodies on blankets, sprawled in tall grass.

Everywhere I looked, traipsing naked
But for my sneakers, allowing my eye
Freedom to stroke each body, I saw girls
Feeding on mouths of boys or boys on boys
And girls on girls in hungry give and take,
An endless feasting no one stinted
Or hoarded.
        The grass shivered, intelligential
As Bruno's planets and stars, sentient
Beings locked in mutual play of love's
Polymorphous energies.
            Cupid's rimes,
Sex slayings in the woods, the fire Bruno's
Inquisitors lit round his ankles, were these
Love's consequences too?
           Tattoos slither down
Neck and shoulders to gnash fangs in hearts,

Copulation thrives!
                    In Eden Adam
Listens to Raphael, blushing, tell how angels
Interpenetrate, steam into steam, lovemaking
Eternal at each gasp.
                    My sneakers smelled
Of pollen, dust, sun, sweat, my armpits ran,
In my desire weeds brushing my legs
Turned to fingers quick, feathery, or thorn-sharp
Nails raking so voluptuously calves and knees
Touch was a dimension of imagination
Greased and rubbed to clawing spasm.

Then Cannibal Love appeared out of the grass:

"Kiss that one's mouth, hold the other one's hand,
And at dawn no anguish, embrace your fate
In bed on top or under your love, be kind
Or cruel, but obey my great command,
Taste me, lovers, sample my gristled heart,
Meat must be devoured by meat, and no bond
Lasts unless I, Love, sit down with you and eat."

Meat Market

Slick of light burning down into my eyes,
        I wanted to escape, to be pure snout,
to nuzzle duff and revel
        in odors rich, stinking, fierce —

part dog, part pig snuffing out truffles,
        I knew my adventuring on behalf of body
would lead back to a window-smashed
        warehouse landscape where what transpired

among rat droppings, fears sprouting like mushrooms in the damp,
        promised body's reckoning with Love:
Stretching away were cattle chutes, gliding meat hooks
        in abandoned lockers, ghost carcasses

strung up by tendons, delicate hooves pathetic and demure.
        Walls buckling were all that was left of the meat market,
where by day slaughter took place on a cash basis,
        and at night trade was handled

in empty loading docks and sheltered concrete bays.
        But like a French cathedral, capitals
carved with sensuous or demonic faces
        emerging from scrolling stone,

a phantom building soared upward through this place of ruin
        penetrated by those massive
arches and buttresses, the stones' weight
        counterbalanced by rose window light tainting

marble flanks of sacred statuary. While trash blew in and out
        of the wrenched off their hinges' doors and gulfs of air
wafted whiffs of sweat and semen, I imagined love cries
        echoing and decaying off the vaulted ceiling—

But only swallows canvassing the air betrayed
        presences lurking in the shadows.
My mind's din split into tones, quarter tones echoing
        and straining into broken music:

Was this what the newly dead must hear, cattle-eyed souls bellowing
        in fear, or hungry, unappeased, wanting more?
. . . Oh body tempted by slough *and* spire, wanting to go down on
        its knees before the altar, blood hammering in its ears.

The Fissure

Your power to make me feel that I am
    I and none other dims like lights going
Out room by room. Just to think of you can seem
    Ridiculous—a hopeless way of hoping
So when I wake from a nap into amnesia
    For a moment, I imagine you sleeping
Here beside me . . . at least till the abyss
    Opens next to my bed . . .
                    Your jeans faded
In the sun's mindless wash, by what slow degrees
    You were taken from me: Baffled
By your absence, who I was when
    I knew you now seems like some outpost isolated
And unreckonable from every known
    Landmark . . .
              I never bothered to conceal
My need of you: I was Scott freezing in
    His tent, my stumbling quest of the Pole
Tireless, but absurd, your magnetic center always
    Moving, and finally, unreachable:
Between dots of photographs infinite space
    Seeps unstoppably: Flash of hair, an eye,
An otherworldly dahlia, a jigsaw puzzle piece,
    Two ghosts shredding into mist, all blurred by
Habit—for how many years did you exert
    Your influence like pressure undersea
That keeps giant crabs' armor from splitting at

The seams?
                    Such armor! My beard a fortress
You saw right through, my green linen suit,
        Fraying now, my studied "fierceness" —
All because I was scared to be seen
        As you saw me: Your dog with muddy paws
Jumping up, too eager, addicted to the tone
        Of your low whistle, our prearranged sign
For the afterlife if a heaven
        Or hell would take us in . . .
                            Your seduction
Of this world, which was convinced you were
        Self-sufficient, took place not in a garden
But in your den of marijuana where
        You and your friend Susan stripped all pretentions
Bare: Such scams I practiced, eager
        To convince X I was worthy as Y to win
The prize honoring "the third most unknown
        Younger older poet never to have been
Recognized by the Pope, the Queen of Sweden,
        And Tony the counterman" — our Elvis
Look-alike who played Elvis's Christmas album
        All year through . . . To a pro like you, all this
Was amateur: Even with Death you were at ease,
        Making him put off his visit's purpose
With your repartee!
                        Now, just to get a glimpse
        Of you, I have to imagine you laughing,
Bemused, clinical, a virologist
        Tracing pathways ceaselessly mutating,
My memory's residue blown down the highway

To Route 16 to potholed streets dead-ending
In warehouse parking lots next to sludgy
    Tidal flats raw and stinking in the sun: There,
In the haze the fissure opens, there, I
    Descend:
                Without you to lead me from upper
Worlds of sodium vapor that lit the shore
    We walked along under your sign, Cancer,
I'm just a tourist gawking at your lower
    Zones of night, the submarine and souterrain
Of dream-sewage, rat tunnel, scum-bottomed harbor
    In which you plunged your own personal Damned,
Miming on the phone their need of you to listen,
    Your voice empathetic even as you yawned . . .
My shadow slips and stumbles down
    Rubble, midnight construction lamps dimly
Haloing my head, my new-shaven
    Face still raw, my legs grazed by
Winged shadows in the fumes billowing
    From that fissure until our sweetly
Interchangeable *We I You* that contain
    And pour us out into the mouths of others
Seeps away into eternal frozen rain:

    At the world's bottom I see you hover
Like fog over polar seas, your presence
    Glinting in footprints across the glacier.
(Of course I don't see you, the image is
    Ripped off from the 1911 encyclopedia you
Would have loved to read if you still had eyes.)
    The flow of seconds is a floe

Of ice hardening round faces that peer
    Past each other into drifting snow.
How far down in the ice shelf they'd have to bore
    To find us, the block of ice we're frozen in
Moving with the ice pack toward open water.

House Beyond the Last Thought

House of attainment that will never be attained,
Attic of bedsprings, innocence of old rags,
Of passé porno novels, *Lust of the Pharaohs,*
Confessions of a San Francisco Street Car Conductor,
Its doors are all open, porch and lintel sag.

House on a street where other houses have collapsed
And only mud-daubed nests remain, purple martins flying
In and out of wrecked eaves, house of tarpaper
Blistering blacker in the sun, in this house of mother
And first love a neuter sweetness clings.

Of stone or flesh, of many houses built over
And over on the same ground, skyscraper shadows toppling
Tenement and tanning factory a hundred years gone,
Structure of mind first roofless, windowless,
Now framed out into joists, rafters, beams.

A cross-stitch daisy or Bauhaus chair, a dog's bowl
Of water, a millrace of shadows treading the worn stair,
House built and unbuilt for an unknown sum,
House no house where no one is home,
Its walls fall beyond any known horizon,

House that's a screen that's a wall that's a screen.

PROLOGUE

In the distance gleams an island,
an island risen fresh
from the ocean overnight,
volcanic slopes
smoking, the thermal vent in the deep
heating the tide already washing and washing
at the congealing lava.

By noon, love will have planted the rock
with vineyards, hydrangeas,
ginger lilies overflowing
down the crater where
water gathers instead of magma.
The oars carved from cedar limbs will already have found
their way into the historical society's
tottering museum, next to the vitrine
of stuffed songbirds, chloroformed butterflies, and the two-headed
calf staring off in both directions, its eyes
focused on the skeleton of a nearly extinct species
of whale and, obversely,
the azulejos of a man strumming
a lute, his manner all languor and sensual ease
while Venus lounges naked next to a pool.

By evening, the island will have
washed away. Only ancient charts and maps
will record its coordinates while
the water where it lay negligently
shines above the light-starved
face of the ocean bottom.

—I come to you with a joke about the monkey and the lion,
the lion chasing the monkey across a desert island . . .
and when you laugh, the monkey
takes off his sunglasses, the lion looks pleased
that the monkey has deceived him,
                              and light
strokes the creases
in your oxblood leather jacket.

I

It's right, isn't it, to see
it all as choice? to see in you the structure
of desire inside us both
at work in the parking lot
when you hunch
in your leather jacket
wind-thrashed and sun-beaten?

The tide seems like a counterforce;
in its own gathering
that flings us out,
we're secondary — its dailiness
our fate we're swept into
but quietly, the hours
worn threadbare
by my periodic fevers,
then patched back together
in thick-headed sleep
my pillow insists on and softens:

That motion
absorbs us the way islands in
the tide surface
and sink . . . taut
sea, scarps and grooves, blasted
craters loom reliable
as clothes wearing day by day
to rags.

2

Despite my weakness, my predilection
for sudden sweats,
you still want to take me away
from the cold spots
hollowing out my bed? a chill
relished all the more for your sudden warmth . . .

What's that subtlety of scent pervading
me, getting behind
all my evasions, my careful and my reckless,
my cunning rationales
for resisting you?

Aren't I hoping to see a version
of love that isn't overlaid
with desire dribbling, cringing . . . a love that shrugs off
the sweating body?

I can't say Yes or No
to you without feeling
the current drag
me which way it must, though
secretly, insidiously . . . its seadrift
your gift of inertia to move
me where you wait, a like casualty
of fathoms no light
penetrates in the blind
wide elemental salt where
we hesitate.

3

Below the faintly
humming clock
two people lie stranded
in a bed, the bed
a seismograph of speech
                    that registers the shock
of hearing themselves say
Yes . . .

        And No
rifts the cooling dark.

4

"My health is . . ."

"I completely understand —
the fact that you might be . . .
Look, it doesn't matter."

(A well-meant lie we both consent to:
You fold the umbrella, hang it
on its hook, then wrap your faded scarf —
the scarf you stole from me, the last thing
I ever imagined *you*
would want to wear — around
my neck.)

5

Your lover says to you, "You're skin and bones."

What your lover means seems transparent:

You're a kind of death's head
that ought to have the sense
to hide itself from sight.

But you look in the mirror and the mirror says:

"Wayward, trusting, amiable flesh, flesh
lending itself to other flesh,
how can you help but be seduced by another's body?"

6

We sailed past known markers of our world,
pleasure was the expanse we crossed, pleasure
without bottom or limiting dimension;

always it's enacted as a possibility
in even our most familiar glance
or habit-ridden touch—
                              until its deferral,
when my body falls ill—
which stings
as a reproach, a judgment on me . . .

Though not a judgment, really,
nothing so grand . . . just what happens when I feel you
staring at me,
                    scared by what you see;
as if death and sickness, pleasure and health
were either side of a comma
balanced neatly as opposites . . .
                                        at least until your hand,
warm on mine, arouses me:
                              My mind
turns on but my skin turns
cardboard, my clammy weakness
turning you
away . . .
              my body's garbled syntax
mixing pain with pleasure,

                            pleasure with pain
splayed on both sides of that comma . . .

If only the gap that comma
fills, the silence it invokes and wills into being,
would breathe
the breath of given and taken pleasure
or reveal how in sickness
incubates the health we long for . . .

— And so we suffer our ignorance.

7

The sick body reproaches purity of form?
Purity demands passion —
and all we have to offer is our straying affection,
the sour facts of my convalescing body . . .

While we watch wing pass into wing at each embrace,
the gods' ichor mingling, vapor into vapor,
we sit reading our separate books, apart
together, the digital clock's numbers
vanishing into blackness, gravity holding us
as we prefer to be held, you still you, me me . . .

Was it you, in the end, who left me?
Or was the ice on my brow too thick
for me to wipe away?

8

The face
of our attraction was a high dune
that overlooked the ocean—perfectly bare,
featureless from a distance,
up close you could see every groove and windrow:

Its bareness became an essential condition of our love—

by sun and wind scoured,
the dune's contour held its shape,
each single grain blown off from the hardpan
swirling back when the wind shifted direction:

The dune's configuration promised coherence in systems
of wind and wave and sun
that by effort our love could duplicate . . .

But the high singleness of that dune's
wide stare pierced us every morning
and every night:

There was no escape from its invincible erosion—
and that too became part of what we loved,
no matter how barren or exposed.

9

The quiet delirium of waking;

and then, hours later,
the cool abyss of sleep.

Between, my love is an absence; a renunciation
so thorough
it feels like the arms
of virtue.

But such virtue isn't flesh remembered
the way I remember you . . .

How unredeemable sex is — especially
the presumption that what we hunger for
can be summoned up by being tossed to coma
in each other's arms.

10

Scar of lost love so tender to finger and rub
until it bleeds,
he couldn't help himself,
it became a compulsion — he was

Scott in his tent, writing in his journal until his beard froze over, face
covered
by a mask of ice,
the Pole become the axis of his being;

or else he was descending into the underworld in search of
his Persephone, Enkidu, his Eurydice —
the darkness mirroring his face
endlessly, angle on angle of cheekbones, eyes staring at their own

features swarming . . .

And "he" whom you saw through
and called by name, my name,
as you lay in the dark veins
of silt and clay and looked past or beyond or into some distance

I couldn't understand, you were kind
to my incapacity, you forgave me my lack
of knowing the limits of your love.

After rain the maple dying from the top
down, drop and drop
shed from its scaly branches, gleams
with soft afternoon light that is merely light.

Nothing has passed between us but time.

As if the ceiling were a mirror,
the room momentarily brightens
with a cool crystalline
shine glinting
off the tip of my pen.

(Had we lasted
we would have told our good and bad days, felt harassed
together, fought and digressed
into sweat and candlewax, old tenderness
kneaded into pliancy.)

The days pass in a sequence
neither a lover nor a fool to be spurned
would recognize as passion so slow
on the axis of my looking does your face,
untranced and clear, turn.

Vessel

Branching the way blind fingers splay across
The face they're reading, trees trace the backyard
Ditch so that their shadows drop off into
Space,
      an abyss where I hear a neighbor boy's
Voice cursing an exhilarated, out of its mind,

Unappeasably inventive flow of
"Fuck fuck motherfuck" ecstasy that maybe
He imagines the neighborhood can't hear? —
                              or is his tongue wired
To some source of inspired but as yet unknown
Intelligence that radiates from all of us and he

Is its mouthpiece, speaking it to the trees
That screen him from me listening to his
Unrelenting arias, predestined like birdsong
Flowing unbidden, of four-letter almost
Erotic keening over something I know too,

Everybody knows? —
                    and even if all it is
Is the "fuck fuck motherfuck" ecstasy
Of April budding in his mouth and sending down
Roots to some anti-self that sprouts and shadows
Him as it croons and shouts the song of its difference —

Even then, this Billy whom I don't think twice about
When we meet in the alley and slap palms
Or I see him playing alone on the swings or big kids' slide,
Even then is he the vessel

                    of some signal that uses us,
Down in the abyss irradiating him so that just this instant

      Whatever that other uses him for he can't resist:
His voice an instrument of blissed-out torment
Until that grip flings him loose —
Who knows which of us it chooses to penetrate
Next, making us suddenly sweat or shiver,

That influence bathing everything budding
                        in profane rays.

This Day Only

Whether we are or aren't immortal, whether we know
who pulls the strings or it's this day only that the light falls
inexhaustibly, the whole prison feeling of too much

within too little dissolves into sun
scaling the telephone pole. On a morning this calm,
Medusa's midnight mask of stone is only a snarl

of kite string marooned in the maple's crown . . .
Everyone's sitting around having a good time,
the table is set with beer and wine, cheese and cake—

between the table slats, ten thousand fathoms down
we sense in your vacuity an intelligence
working us as if we were threads woven on a loom:

To name you is to name the cold that won't relent,
the vertigo, irremediable, that rises up to meet the wings
of a jetliner suspended above the ocean dark.

You bat us this way and that in the heaving atmosphere.
Whatever we do, wherever we are,
we're creeping along the edge of your abyss.

2

Your comings and goings, your heavens and hells.
Your minions rush into the vacuum that attends you,
they hover like the balloons advertising

this Sunday's yard sale, THIS DAY ONLY . . .
July eleventh, the air so clear
I can see to the very bottom of the sky!

You lead me down into your cold that shivers up
through the fur coat wanly sprawled under the balloons,
your depths so precipitous in the swirl of the fur's grain

it's like diving into the gulf between each atom . . .
This morning the leaves are too flagrantly green —
green as the respirator mask Charlie breathes through

on his scaffold, his mask making him look
like a serpent god or simian angel, his white shirt
blending with the wall he's painting

such an insidious white it seems he's being
swallowed stroke by stroke, that whiteness subtle
and ungraspable flowering from the paint can.

3

Zone innavigable of being, unforeseeable zone,
whether you wear a friend's face or grin back at us
from the mirror or the blankness of a computer screen,

every instant I feel you trying to lure me down:
You crackle with feedback from Hendrix's guitar,
empty snail shells reverberate with your cataracting roar.

Everywhere I look this clairvoyant July, between shafts of sun
you insinuate yourself deep into the day:
A man I know is about to die, today, maybe tomorrow;

his voice on the phone is interrupted by your static
as if he were marooned on a mountaintop
or shouted up from the bottom of a crevasse . . .

The rich stink of carrion that wafts from the garden,
slugs indomitably traversing the wet grass,
the couple strolling, their aura frangible, incalculable,

hint at your vibrations both visible and invisible.
Isn't this all part of your ambiguous shining, a blossoming
and withering so particular it can't be argued over?

Out in the Garden

In this flowering denser than ever I
Remember between the leaves a shimmering
Like molten metal announces the arrival

Of spirits from the air, loud partyers,
Unpicturesque, erotic snouts and hair.
Some wear monster masks, but many seem like us,

Smiling, keenly happy to have made their way,
After all these centuries, out into the garden!
Hades, too, is out walking in the garden,

He's come to set up shop with the underworld's
Shy powers under the rotting grape arbor, his lathes
Milling each soul finer than a millionth millimeter!

Hades, my old friend Hades, all of us must
Acknowledge you're still master of your trade,
But take one moment on this delicious

Evening to glance away from your grim work
And down a drink or two. And as for you,
Cerberus, stop your barking and pissing

On these flowers' gorgeous faces — let's hear
Only the calming, triple rhythm of your
Three tongues lapping water in perfect time

To the lulling meter of a neighbor's sprinkler,
Lie down under the trees and let the party
Spill over until the leaves filling in

Make the street invisible behind a wall
Thickening every instant every breath
Plunging into vegetable rot and fiber.

Trees by Firelight

The shapes they make are shapes they hide from day.
As if seeing what we see by night would give
Us nightmares if we saw it clarified by day.
As if our world that they and we inhabit is
Really a world of shadowy forms suggestive
Of antlers flickering from our brows in the hiddenness
Of our own natures giving themselves away.

The human figures in the windows at the party
Next door, mammalian croonings, touchings, the current
Of courtship that plays across the dark the way fire
Plays across a log, do these figures know, or maybe
They don't know that just behind or in front a shadowy
Creeping adheres to their footsteps, inescapable
As the fire's shadows creeping across the wall?

Looming on the flame's far side is a void
Of tree shadows mimicking the beak of a bird
Pecking, then jabbing whenever the breeze
Lifts. The beak pecks into the dark a script
Like braille, but no matter how we try to turn
Ourselves or the darkness inside out, the dots
Are punched into the side of the paper we can't feel . . .

Now the flame abstracts another tree
To waves blowing up in exponential fury, the ship's
Prop not turning fast enough to breast the water wall
Driving the prow under, rupturing the hull, the cargo
Signaling from the deep . . . A month ago, two months now,
At my cousin's funeral I sat before the gas fire in the funeral home's
Parlor and listened to a man tell me business was booming:

His penis pumps and prostheses and sex toys
Were all the highest quality, and if ever I needed a dungeon
Or dungeon master/mistress trained in safe S & M,
"My dungeons are floor to ceiling mirrors, everything
Spotless, antiseptic; our people are all bonded,
We don't do anything with children or animals,
But we've got whatever else you and the missus want."

Once upon a time we slept out on the hard ground,
We were dreamless, artless, our minds blank as stone.
Against the other gods' wills, a god stole for us
Divine fire, they chained him to a cliff, a vulture
Swooped down each noon to eat his liver that grew
Back overnight while our fires kept us warm,
Our backs to the shadowy corners of the house.

Ars Poetica: My Mother as
Oedipus at Colonus

Not precisely heroic, not tragic
    or untragic, no vanquisher
        of Sphinxes, no fated self-blinder, but Oedipus

shorn of Poetry, stuck forever
    with that ridiculous name—
        Swollenfoot hobbling to the precipice:

her version of Oedipus had its own peculiar
    dignity: exile, cunning, she learned from death
        and poverty—but death as simply there,

poverty there, the way other people's backyards and gardens are . . .
    Ghosts whispering at the edges of
        her day taught her

her own brand of poetry: Skeptic of hope, suspicious
    of mother-love's pure
        Abstract, she learned to speak

as a prophet of the concrete linked
    by pain to the past. While playing out roles
        of teacher, mother, she sat alone

in her mind's theater
    and strove to devise her own secret grammar
        that would speak in a syntax suitable to her passion . . .

Never did she say to the gods
        that hastened to destroy her
            or to the gods that she hastened to destroy:

— *I want my father and mother/wife never to have died.*

— *I want my children to look at me unashamed.*

— *I want back the sight of my eyes that I myself put out.*

As she stepped back from a world in which
        her actions could no longer be
            contained (she'd seen

the abyss flashing among
        the pots and pans) — her estrangement seemed
            double-bladed as her freedom; her freedom

to sorrow for the world on the Sphinx-like screen
        confiding its riddle of mutability . . . the Sphinx
            she would have stroked and stroked

until it licked her hand and looked up into her eyes
        the way a pet dog looks into human eyes . . .
            Aging under the knowledge of that look, her heart

grew kind, hopeful, but objective:
        She knew it was late — done with thunder —
            rain warm all day in February's thaw, her words

kept fogging on the glass:
    Forms of expression became forms of experience—
        she spoke aloud the raw division between her story

as just another history and an emblem inventing
    the human, unfurling . . .
        And never did she speak in "the language of gods."

Spring Morning

Hierarchies are coming unstrung. Whoever I am at this moment,
Whoever I might be at the next is suddenly in abeyance:
I've stepped sideways out of cascading white water hesitating
At the waterfall's backward scrambling, horrified-of-falling
Reversal at the instant of the plunge.

                                    A siren cuts through the quiet.
The dog next door barks and barks. Walls between rooms
Grow more and more transparent, there's a buzz and blur
Of spring's first bees before my window.

                                    A sweet sensation
Of feeling myself for this moment immortal is giving way
To an equal gravitational pull impartially
Pulling everything into it.

                            Inside my mood I'm on a battlefield
In a square of infantry, the first row kneeling to fire,
Then falling back as the next row steps forward, kneels, fires,
Our square helplessly advancing no matter that the man
Next to us falls, no matter that our volleys can't be heard
In the void of the battlefield we're slowly crossing.
The smoke is clearing from my eyes.

                                    The developer who planted
Trees in the backyard is out there on a bench reading
The newspaper. He's promised the neighborhood this house is
The house he'll live in forever, but even as he reads, moving men
Carry his rugs and kitchen gadgets out the door.

                                    Who knows

What keeps the trees from appearing to us
As they appear to the lifelong blind stricken

Unexpectedly with sight, blots and flashes of scarifying
Green burning into retinas that see disordered
"A vast vacuity . . . the womb of nature . . . neither sea,
nor shore, nor air, nor fire, / But all these in their pregnant
causes mixed / Confusedly, and which thus must ever fight"
To make green adhere to the leaves' shadowy dip and toss.

Bridge

It wasn't the sort of thing that's talked about;
And we certainly none of us mentioned it to her:
Yet her head had an aspect, an aura almost, of such
Total strangeness inside the white curls
Grown wispy, that it seemed her head hovered
In a fourth dimension in which all our
Assumptions were . . . not only unworkable; but the very
Categories we tried to organize to say things
In a bafflement of unease we could scarcely hide
Were insufficient to the change that had overcome her.
The maddening questions repeated in her sweet, diffident,
I-know-there's-something-wrong-with-me-what-is-it? voice,
"You're Tom, now, aren't you, the son
Of Kenneth?" "Yes, I'm Tom, that's right," began
To erode the outlines of the day: the chair she sat in
Was less definite, the books whose letters in arbitrary
Orders agreed upon to mean *this* not *that* hummed
Discordantly in bookshelves as if the world of mind
Were growing vegetative — topiary shapes
Of custom, convention running wild beyond
Patterns we recognized.
                              The room murmured
In confusion of pity and terror: pity that she
Was loosing her hold on the railing plunging
Out of sight into lower stories of night; terror that
The stair is no longer clearly marked for us,
That we only take for granted our mastery of it

As we effortlessly climb landing to landing, descrying
From one level the means to get to the upper stories:
Climbing the stairs with her as she walks off the steps
Into impenetrable grayness, impenetrable to us
At least, though now her medium, her element,
One of the orders of human being not alien
To her: only the phylum of experience
She participates in. It wasn't revulsion
I felt exactly that someday my mind could be "gone"
Like hers — I didn't, couldn't know what "gone"
Might mean without memory to hold faces
In place, a lifetime's worth of loving or painful
Or half-conscious associations thinning to gray wisps
In graying air; it wasn't that, though that was part —:
Here she was, an able, courageous, pious woman,
Sucking and blowing a little tune on her mouth harp, her face
Joyous as she played "Skip to My Lou," "Red River Valley" . . .
Her eyes, too simply eyes, deflected yours, too luminous
And cool, so detached from her face resembling
Now a palimpsest of all her faces from when
She first bent over her cottage cheese and pears
At recess as a young teacher in a sod-roofed schoolhouse,
Boarding on the farms of pupils, to this moment of her
Fathomless regard forceful as a wind hurling us
Back off the peak where she bivouacked with her walker,
Bible, her Palmer Method letters gently insisting
The Shepherd lead us through the Valley of the Shadow . . .
How clear she had once been!
                                        Was God Himself fading
For her? — He seemed to be — she no longer looked at
Her Bible or asked to go to Services, stranded

On a world we couldn't cross to: the bridge
Spanning the void was being dismantled, girders
Hanging rusted, whole spans wrenching away
And collapsing into nothingness, grinding steel
Mangling itself from its own dead weight crashing
Down and down around her as she sat
Unaware, mouth harp in hand.
                                        We were all
Schoolchildren behind a thick pane of glass
Shouting at our teacher to come in before the dust cloud
Blowing engulfed the plain she was the lone figure
Unsteadily crossing, her frailty oblivious to
What was heaping up on the South South West
Horizon, her head a dwindling point of light isolated
In noon twilight while in the stillness before the wind's moan
Dogs barked, barked, birds madly sang and cattle
In pens balked, spooked, bellowing for their wayward calves.

For Robert Owen Sleigh,
P.F.C., 100th Division

The men you killed with a grenade that day
Come back in dreams: Gold-epauletted conductor
Punching your ticket on a train, black-vested waiter

Bowing to recite "The house specials."
But it was your own story, not some "war story,"
You wanted me to understand . . . the way

Going to the dump after the War made you
Feel at home — among gulls scavenging, foxes
And raccoons rummaging all night . . .

Red light leaking from behind your window shade:
Color of the murdered dead's blood.
Midnight ashtray smoking, butts heaped and twisted

In a mounting pile . . . Their voices rising in
Your throat, the old warriors try to speak:
Sitting Bull, Achilles, Colonel Zaner

Who ordered you to follow him across
An open field, bullets kicking up divots
At your feet. In your underwear and T-shirt

Lit by the refrigerator light, you grope
For the ice water, lay the sweating pitcher
Against your sweating face, your voice's deadpan

Harrowing my ear: As a German soldier approached
Through mist, you bent to tie your boots,
So scared you knotted the laces together

And tripped when you leaped out of the foxhole,
Your M-1 sliding into the mud at the man's feet.
He handed you your rifle, turning the barrel

Toward his chest the way someone passing
A butter knife holds it out handle first.
"Danke schön," you said; "Bitte sehr," his reply,

Holding out his wrists to be bound: Your eyes ambushing mine,
You shrugged, ". . . and they gave me the Bronze Star."
Surrender to memory freshens your absence

Wafting from your fading uniform.
You let me put it on when I was a boy,
The sleeves so long they seemed to dangle

In defeat, gravity so heavy in the pockets
The coat could have been the uniform
Of all the dead barracked in together . . .

Voice from an empty bottle echoing
Among the darkened rows of bunks, make the dead
Lie still! Colonel Zaner, Sitting Bull, Achilles . . .

Forever in Elysium I see them standing by you
Listening to how you ran across that field,
Swearing under your breath but obediently loyal

To that "fire-eating old fool." Survivor
Whose voice is balm, casualty of time
My voice can't plumb, oh huddler

In foxholes, happy eater of K-ration
Chocolate bars, scoffer and stumbler, come out
Of the pickle barrel in the bomb-blasted cellar:

The SS man, his Luger drawn, lies dead
On the splintered stairs and there's a hole
Blown through the wall just your shape and size.

In rudeness, wildness of bird and undergrowth,
like pilgrims wayfaring
in a wilderness dense, tangled, shadowy, we came to visit her
and sheltered in the waiting room while she,
bareheaded, blended white on white in the snowed-in wood:

At times pain and bewilderment drove her from her thicket
and she clutched
the bed frame and talked, talked — but what her eyes told was
her embarassment
at how her cancer should make her cry out

like a Shakespearean hero, "O world!" when what she wanted
was no self-drama,
to ask others how they were; to simply smile at everyone else's
jokes; to sip nonchalantly
her special tea, and cease upon the midnight

while Keats's nightingale poured forth its soul abroad
with requisite ecstasy.
The more you watched her though, the more you lost your way:
the path her thinking
and being wandered down foundered into brambles

or seeped into sunless tarns sunken in hollows:
Elaine
of the movie queen wide-brimmed hats, nerves ridden by powers
her willed extravagance
of patience and calm could no longer contain,

Elaine who walked in her own spirit world where
Archetypes
in evening wear traded banter about the affair between
Nothing and All,
this Elaine, soft-spoken and courteous,

her nature kind, stoic, embraced by the Abstract,
kept stumbling
and falling behind the other Elaine
driven through
the wood by errant impulse.

The once living forest hardened around her
to insensate lumber
and forced her to the banks along the icy river where we
in our seeming
health, according to custom, pretended

to be picnicking—but our words barely carried
to the bank she grew out of,
the lone thinking reed on her side of the water . . .
And as we watched,
a trick of perspective though not a trick,

just the condition of knowledge her change rooted in,
like Daphne
in reverse, a tree growing human, she sprouted up higher
and towered over us:
"Men that look upon my outside, perusing only

my condition, and fortunes, do erre in my altitude; for I am above
Atlas his shoulders."
And among the branches unmoving high above us as we traveled on,
the nightingale
kept silent, barely rustling its wings.

Amores, II, vi

after Ovid

It's dead, poor thing, our parrot from the Indies
Where dawn first wakened Polly to our talk.
Dear Polly, old Polly, we could never figure out
If we were right in thinking you a "he"?
Each day you mimicked back our silly "Polly want a cracker?,"
Rasping it out pitch-perfect, with real style.
Now, in just one night, your feathers start to fade.

Philomela, listen: If you're still weeping over
What Ismarus did to you, weep at this too:
You've more than served your term of grief;
And besides, your pain lies buried in the past,
Turn those tears for Itys to this brilliant bird's
Plight, join the song of his fellow creatures
Winging faithfully to his funeral rites —
Wings beating breasts, talons tearing plumes,
Whistles sadder than the bugle playing "Taps."
And sadder than all the rest, your old friend
The mourning dove moans and moans — all your lives
The two of you together; Pylades to Orestes
No more loving and true.
                              But what does friendship matter
Now, or your gorgeous feathers, what did your skill
In talking the way we do, alert and exact
To all our varied tones, a genius of a bird, really,
In giving our words back, oh what good
Did your gift do, so pleasing to my Corinna

The moment she heard you? Your wings' luster
Made emeralds green with envy, your beak's
Punic red and saffron outshone rubies and gold.
Bird, glory of the hovering, clear air,
You've fallen back to earth forever.

Envy, I guess, took aim and struck you down, you
Who wouldn't hurt a fly. Talk talk talk
Was your delight, not like quail who bicker
Day in day out the same as old married couples
Stewed in their petty, long-lived quarrels.
To make much of little was your art:
Talk talk talk you loved so well you hardly
Took a moment to crack a nut. A few poppyseeds,
You fell fast asleep; a drop or two of pure water
Soothed your throat.
                              The greedy vulture keeps on
Swooping down, hawks circle on thermals high up
In the air, jackdaws continue forecasting rain,
And the raven, hated by Minerva in her
Lustrous armor, has nine lives to lead
Before meeting up with Fate. All these thrive,
But you, parrot, virtuoso of our divinely human speech,
Brought to us here from where the world ends,
You've flown beyond our power to call you back—
It's always like this, Fate snatches up the best
While the worst take their own sweet time.
Protesilaus died, and guess who stood around
Lounging by his grave? Thersites, that's who.
And Hector too, dragged in the dust,
Fed the vultures while Paris looked on.

And why remember my love's prayers and vows
For you, her devotions swept out to sea by a southern gale.
On the seventh dawn, the last you'd ever see,
Fate had spun your thread right to the end
But words still leaped into your dying throat,
"Corinna, farewell, farewell, farewell . . ."

In Elysium, at the bottom of a hill, a grove
Of oaks perpetually shades moist earth
Sprouting grass that glistens always green.
Here, if what we know to doubt is ever true,
Birds like you flock together, and vultures
And raptors out of instinct keep away.
Here swans glide on their pure reflections,
The phoenix rises from its ashes, the only one
Of its kind, the peacock of Juno spreads
For her pleasure those feathers in the sun,
And the dove nestles in the plumage of her lover.
This will be our dear bird's home, his human words
Luring all the rest to listen.
                              And over his bones
A little tomb, tomb so small it's just his size,
Will be built for him, with a homely slate stone
Just large enough to say:
                              This says all there is
To say about how much she misses me, I who spoke
With skill beyond a bird's Corinna's loving words.

III

To Water

Element so clear, element of grace
    Moving so quickly the moving seems at rest,
If you had being other than this blur

    Of surface passing into surface, your
Body would take shape as her body does
    So constant in its flowing otherness

Outward toward this instant depending
    And falling into depths where all is flowing
Toward this stasis that is her hand

    Lifting to her hair, hesitating, no sound
Or movement more present to my watchfulness—
    Not time, hope, afternoons that drift like ash,

Not sweat, sperm, spit or sighs, not blood on sheets
    Or sheets rippling over flesh, no movement
Moves like her hand's gentle unmoving

    While wherever you will flow keeps flowing.

Long Illness

Ten thousand fathoms down: The self a Mindanao Trench, and in
   that trench
As from a porthole in a bathysphere, an observer, pure eyeball

Witnesses devils, demons, their confessions too intricate
To follow . . . cattle prods, bathtubs full of ice, a matchbook and
   a needle,

Will and heart debased, pleasure in terror mounting to exaltation:
Burn, burn, strip everything away, reduce it to increate nothing!

Then, brightening, like a bubble surfacing, expanding,
A water glass refracts sunlight across a tablecloth,

The light so clear as to be almost painful: Overself
Spying on self crying out in pain, pathetic, reduced to howling,

Mewing; then words inside of fever mutating into nonsense rhymes,
Never-ending logorrhea, then an autism immune

To terror whispering in the dark: Out the window,
Tainted by scaly bark and snow melting from the gutter

Snow clouds massing over the city's flashing beacons
Boil into themselves: Open up your eyes, open them!

The couch burns away beneath the sleeping body,
Ash and magma harden round the head and neck,

Flow downward over torso, arms, legs
. . . Turn over now, turn over if you can, the fire's an illusion,

It's only what I'm seeing there on the table: Where are you, Ellen,
Who held that glass an hour or so ago, and left it there distilling

Afternoon light into this isolate clear shining
That is yours in your absence, that is your touch

Remembered on my sweating face haunted by
Your coming close, the room laboring in sleep.

What Can Be Said

Pylons of moonlight strum through the night.

Windows line up in dusk-drained grids.

Dogs sniff garbage
in a hundred alleys, crosses
tarnish atop gravestones and churches.
City lights, molten inside
their blank dominion, reach beyond
their own inchoate shining
to tinge the gulf opening round the moon
half risen, jets
slicing that nimbus.

What can be said under such influence?

That the day, lived through in obdurate passion,
as I live with you,
never lapses into oblivion, some wisp
or granule of care outlasting
even the coffin or crematory fire?

Moon so full in scarred, quiet abandonment,
what can be said under such influence?

Tonight, collapsing piers, barbwire rusting
and macadam crumbling
shine in its potholed light.

In absences and voids that mimic
gulfs opening round splintering stars,
adventurers of flesh and ruined mind
set out toward home half drunk from the bars;
and as they fare forward, won't some of them
put on the mask
of old man Oedipus chanting
blind on the road to Colonus, their words
fated, ecstatic, self-reviling,
printing like x-rays
on the clouds' subconscious?

Inside this poem's grid of letters,
place of risk and consignment of my will,
here I want to make you invulnerable
to Apollo, who taunts Oedipus,

Now that I, a god, have destroyed you,
what do you most want?

The old man answers, dignified, defiant,

Don't steal from me my child.

And all the while the city holds steady,
city that never goes fully dark
though extinguished light by light.

Amores, III, ix
Ovid

Achilles' mother grieves over her poor boy's body,
And Memnon's mother too weeps for her dead child —
If even goddesses touched by death, though they
Themselves can never die, mourn fates of human sons,
Elegy, ungrateful one, whose name proves all too true,
Unpin your hair, why don't you, and weep for Tibullus
Burning even now on this high-built pyre,
Tibullus who served you with his skill in song.

Venus' loving son stares into the flames,
His quiver turned upside down, arrows broken,
Snapped in two his bow, torch guttering out.
His wings droop and shake from crying the way a child cries,
Feet stumbling, halting, fist beating his heaving chest.
When his brother Aeneas died, they say, and he stepped
Out of Iulus' house, sharing the boy's grief
At his father's last rites, he looked the same as now,
Tears glistening in his hair, utterly undone.
Venus wept no harder for Adonis gored by
The boar's tusk than she does for Tibullus.
People call us poets sacred, watched over by the gods —
Some even say a god takes up residence inside us,
That we're the home of the divine . . .
                                        but death,
Unresting death, goes about his business, laying
A hand so heavy on everything he touches
That all we once thought sacred, held close to us in love,

He spoils, defiles, turning our world to graceless sorrow.
What good was it to Orpheus that Apollo
Was his father, his mother one of the Muses,
And that his singing, masterful as a god's, made
Lions and bears lie down in rapture at his feet—
What good did it do him?

                  And Apollo's other child,
Linus, death seized him too, left his father
Crying out deep in woods where no one might hear,
Linus, Linus, hoping to waken the strings of the numb lyre.
And Homer from whom poets drink as from the Muses' spring,
Our source of song forever, he's gone too, dragged down
Into Avernus deeper than the ocean floor.
The story of suffering at Troy, the weaving unweaving
On the sly at night—only a poet's song outlasts
The hungry fire:

              Delia, Tibullus was first in love
With you, and then with you, Nemesis—neither name
Will ever fade . . .

               What's the point of sacrifice or plucking
The sistrum in honor of Isis or holding back
From our lovers' arms out of devotion to the Goddess?
When Fate sweeps the board with the back
Of his clumsy hand, knocking over the good
And pure the same as the depraved—

                        pardon me,
No one dares to say it—

                then I doubt that gods exist.
Lead a life of prayer—they'll say prayers when you die.
Observe with due respect the gods' offices and rites—
And just as you leave the altar, a hand heavy

And officious drags you from temple to the tomb.
Or put your faith in song, beautiful, intricate—
Then look at Tibullus, his body burned away
To a few double handfuls of clinkers and ashes
His slender urn swallows up, ignorant of
His genius devoted to the Muse.
                                        Tibullus,
Is it you, really you, the flames so hungrily
Devour, unafraid even to feed upon your heart?
Flames so senseless and reckless would burn down
The gods' gold temples—
                                Venus, even on the height of Eryx,
Turns her eyes from this fire; some say not even she
Can keep back her tears for you.
                                        You might have suffered
Worse, of course, when death stalked you in Phaeacia
And threatened to throw your corpse, nameless,
In mean foreign ground. Here, at least your mother
Could close your feverish eyes the moment
Your strength failed; now, she brings your ashes
Offerings, and your sister, by her side, she too
Could share a brother's suffering, a mother's grief,
Her hair unbound about her face, hand beating her breast.
And Nemesis, and your lover before her, both
Could add their kisses to your sister's and mother's,
Their love burning brighter than the crackling pyre,
Delia sighing, "When we were lovers, the flame
Between us burned neither too high nor too low—
When I tended the flame, you burned at the right heat."
And Nemesis replied: "Why do you grieve for Tibullus,
Tibullus was mine — dying, he reached out to take my hand."

If anything remains of us but a name and shadow,
And if the valley of Elysium welcomes poets home,
You'll dwell there with them, Tibullus;

                              and you, Catullus,
So skillful in the art, ivy crowning your temples
Forever youthful, you and your dear Calvus
Will come to meet our Tibullus, and you too, Gallus —
I won't believe the gossip that you betrayed a friend —
You'll greet him too, lavish in your heart's affection,
Spirits always sanguine.

                    Your shade and theirs,
If shades really outlast flesh, will be companions
Forever, and Tibullus, your gentle goodness
Will shine out . . . even there, among the always shining blessed.
— Bones, lie quiet, I pray, in the urn's long embrace,
And may the earth weigh lightly on your ashes.

To Dust

Dust reverses itself and shapes itself into a body—

the water is sweet to it and it comes to the water
wanting, and wanting, goes away, goes away filled
with the fullness of wanting. The body of dust

that finds love in wanting and that once was nothing
remembers the water and its weight, recalls each drop
saturating the dust it sinks down into

now, aroused on its knees, under your gaze.